UNDERSTANDING PERSONAL INJURY IN OKLAHOMA

A Step-by-Step Guide To Damage Recovery

ATTORNEY JOE CARSON

Jacobs & Whitehall
73-03 Bell Blvd, #10
Oakland Gardens, NY 11364
(888) 570-7338
www.jacobsandwhitehall.com
Ordering Information:

Quantity sales. Special discounts are available on quantity purchases by corporations, associations, and others. For details, contact the publisher at the address above.

Orders by U.S. trade bookstores and wholesalers. Please contact Jacobs & Whitehall: Tel: (888) 991-2766 or visit www.jacobsandwhitehall.com.

Printed in the United States of America

Published in 2021

ISBN: 978-1-951149-75-8

Dedication

This book is dedicated to all of my past clients who have taught me how to work hard and care for people in a way that I never dreamed possible. Thank you for trusting me with your case in the awful times after your tragic event. Without my past clients, I would not have the knowledge, ability, and skill to do what I do.

DISCLAIMER

This publication is intended to be used for educational purposes only. No legal advice is being given, and no attorney-client relationship is intended to be created by reading this material. The author assumes no liability for any errors or omissions or for how this book or its contents are used or interpreted, or for any consequences resulting directly or indirectly from the use of this book. For legal or any other advice, please consult an experienced attorney, or the appropriate expert, who is aware of the specific facts of your case and is knowledgeable in the law in your jurisdiction.

WARHAWK LEGAL
127 NW 10th Street
Oklahoma City, OK 73103
(405) 397-1717
www.warhawklegal.com
joe@warhawklegal.com

TESTIMONIALS

"I could not be more impressed with Attorney Joe Carson and his team from Warhawk Legal. My wife and I had a car accident in the Tulsa area and dealt with a lot of stress and anxiety due to our accident. Not only because of the injuries but because of the other driver's insurance companies lack of responsibility in this case. Joe was able to put our minds at ease in regards to what the true outcome should be. Beyond that, Joe and his team really worked in a very professional and timely manner to bring our case to a fair conclusion. We were able to shed away the stress of medical bills and return to a normal way of life. I would recommend Warhawk Legal to anyone that is looking for a fair shake by a professional and moral law firm."

D.T.

****

"LIFE IS UNPREDICTABLE!! And YOU NEVER KNOW!! It just happened. After my wreck, I felt lucky to be alive, but there are also other material things that you must go over. I am glad that Joe Carson from Warhawk legal took over my case and finished it with amazing results! I got more than I expected and my patience was paid back. He is the one who is truly fighting for you and the one who you can trust 100%! Let him work, and he will show you how great a job he and his team can do! I highly recommend him. It's great to share my good experiences with this company. Thank you so much!!!"

- L.P.

****

"Had a great experience with Warhawk Legal. They took care of me from the day I first called them about advice on my case, until we settled my case 2 years later. I would have been lost without their expertise and experience. I highly recommend Joe Carson and his team, they will take care of you all the way through your ordeal "

– J.M

****

"Simply put, I love working with Joe! He has helped me and my husband with a couple different cases. He is very knowledgeable in his field, and he is very patient to explain the reason why yes and why no. A big thank you to this firm for their trustworthiness and confidence in the handling of my case."

– L.J.

****

"Simply phenomenal from start to finish. We could not have had a kinder and more considerate lawyer than Joe. The whole legal team has been responsive, professional, and empathic throughout our court needs."

– P.S.

****

Table Of Contents

i.	Dedication	3
ii.	Disclaimer	4
iii.	Testimonials	5
iv.	About The Author	10
1.	What Is Personal Injury Law In Oklahoma?	14
2.	First Steps That I Need To Take To Give My Case The Best Possible Outcome	21
3.	Factors That Make A Personal Injury Case Viable	27
4.	How Does Comparative Negligence Affect A Personal Injury Case?	33

5.	Insurance That May Be Applicable In Oklahoma	39
6.	Will The Insurance Company Have Access To My Past And Present Medical History?	46
7.	Insurance And Defense Attorneys' Strategies To Avoid Paying Clients	50
8.	How Do You Decide Whether Or Not To Settle A Personal Injury Case?	53
9.	What Factors May Cause My Personal Injury Case To Go To Litigation?	57
10.	Common Mistakes People Make In A Personal Injury Claim	67
11.	Do I Really Need A Lawyer?	71

12.	**If I Hire Joe Carson To Be My Lawyer, What Happens Next?**	**76**
13.	**Frequently Asked Questions**	**80**
14.	**Results Joe Carson Has Achieved For His Clients**	**104**
v.	**Index**	**109**
vi.	**Notes**	**111**

About The Author

Joe Carson was born and raised in Yukon, OK. He graduated from Oklahoma State University with a BS in Environmental Science and a Minor in Agriculture Economics. He received his Juris Doctor from Oklahoma City University in 2002. He is a member of the Oklahoma Bar Association, Oklahoma Association for Justice, and the Oklahoma County Bar Association, as well as the William J. Holloway, Jr. American Inn of Court and the American Association of Justice. He has been named to the Super Lawyer by his peers and has spoken on many topics in his industry, including (1) truck accident litigation, (2)

how to pick a jury, (3) Building Your Civil Trial Skills, Oklahoma Civil Discovery, (4) Challenges for Cause and Making Them Stick, and (5) Plaintiff's Personal Injury from Start to Finish. Joe was recently selected to OCU Law School Executive Board.

Joe has been practicing law in Oklahoma and across the United States for 18 years. His practice is primarily limited to personal injury and wrongful death cases arising from semi wrecks, car wrecks, motorcycle wrecks, airplane wrecks, defective products, and medical errors. Joe also handles insurance bad faith cases, as well as environmental and oil and gas litigation.

Who Is This Book For and Why I Wanted To Write It?

This book was written to hopefully help people better understand the personal injury process. I've been practicing personal injury law in the state of Oklahoma for 18 years. Through assisting a multitude of clients and litigating a large number of cases, I have come to realize that most Oklahomans don't understand their rights when faced with a personal injury incident. Furthermore, I have discovered that the majority of clients don't realize the personal injury claim process is often long, tedious, and difficult. Many clients aren't aware of the numerous factors that contribute to successful claim resolution and the unexpected pitfalls that can occur along the way as we move toward that goal.

Wouldn't it be great if an attorney could simply file a claim and receive money almost immediately upon filing? That would be ideal for everyone. Unfortunately, that is not the way it works.

After explaining the process to each and every client over the years, I have come to the conclusion that every Oklahoman should know what goes into a personal injury claim and what their rights are under Oklahoma law should they ever be faced with this situation.

Things unfortunately happen. Terrible things. Tragic things. Unexpected things. I don't wish any of what has happened to my clients on anyone. And most of what my clients face have long-term results that can permanently alter their lives. There is also the emotional aspect of an injury. To clients, a personal injury is, well, personal. And it should be. Although these types of cases can be emotional, at some point in your case you will be forced to make very hard decisions about what you have experienced. One of the hardest jobs I do is to explain the problem objectively to help the client make a decision without relying on emotion. My hope is this book sheds light on the importance of putting your emotions aside when dealing with your personal injury case.

While the health of my clients is my top priority, I am also here to ensure they are compensated for all of their economic, and non-economic, damages and to walk with them through the process.

This handbook does just that. It is a walk-through, breaking down the stages of a personal injury claim in a generalized manner. Consider it an overview of some of the principals that may affect your claim put forth in a way that is easy to follow and understand. My hope is that it will answer questions, clear up confusion, and shed light on the overall process.

CHAPTER 1

WHAT IS PERSONAL INJURY LAW IN OKLAHOMA?

Personal injury law in Oklahoma is the area of law that covers accidents and injuries, caused by others, that cause you physical or emotional harm. Other than personal injury, Oklahoma law has historically recognized other types of harm to an individual, such as damage to property or damage to one's reputation. The following list includes only a few of the situations in which we have successfully pursued compensation for individuals: Vehicle Wrecks, Trucking Wrecks,

Motorcycle Wrecks, Medical Negligence, Nursing Home Negligence, Wrongful Death, Pedestrian Accidents, Bicycle Accidents, Dog Bites, Premises Liability, Product Liability, Construction Accidents, Workers' Compensation, and Aviation Law.

While the State of Oklahoma is a wonderful place to live and enjoy life, unfortunately, bad things can and do happen. According to the Oklahoma Highway Safety Office (OHSO) which compiles crash data from all law enforcement agencies in Oklahoma, there were 12,304 people injured in car crashes in 2019, and it is worth noting that that this figure may not be all inclusive since there is a likelihood that some crashes with minor injuries aren't reported to law enforcement. Sadly, 640 lives were taken in Oklahoma car crashes in 2019. Of those injured in Oklahoma crashes in 2019, 3,685 people were injured in Oklahoma County, Cleveland County, and Canadian County. Those statistics, including those from the Oklahoma City Metro, include crashes related to speed, alcohol, drugs, distracted drivers, and drowsy drivers to name a few; 291 injuries were speed related, 183 injuries were alcohol related, 39 injuries were drug-related, 408 injuries were related to distracted driving, and 45 injuries were related to drowsy drivers. Holiday travel is a time where travel frequency increases, which increases the frequency of crashes. On New Year's Day of 2018, there were 129 crashes involving injuries or fatalities. Furthermore, during the 2018 Christmas season, there were 166 crashes involving injuries or fatalities. These harrowing statistics suggest Oklahomans should maintain attentiveness, sobriety, and always be on the defense while behind the wheel.

When you or a family member is injured due to the negligence of another, there are multiple categories of monetary damages for which you may be compensated relating to the lasting and sometimes permanent effects of the injury. When one is injured, he or she may need to consult a medical professional and may have to undergo surgery and/or treatment. You have to pay for doctor's visits, prescriptions, surgeries, and treatments. The injured person may be prescribed medicines, may have to take off work, may be unable to perform the same work they did before the injury, or may have to pay for a funeral under less fortunate circumstances. All of those products and services will cost money, and the cost of healthcare continues to grow. It will be challenging to make doctor visits, have surgeries performed, or recover while continuing to work, so you may be forced to take time off and could lose wages you would have otherwise earned had you not been injured. Monetary damages are also known as economic damages and are intended to compensate the injured party for expenses incurred as a result of the injury. An injury from an accident such as a vehicle wreck may cause life-changing injuries that you carry for an extended period of time.

You may also be entitled to non-economic damages such as physical pain and suffering and/or mental pain and suffering. Physical pain and suffering refers to the actual physical pain resulting from the plaintiff's injuries. Emotional pain and suffering refers to the mental toll the injuries have taken on the plaintiff. For example, mental anguish, emotional distress, loss of enjoyment of life, anxiety, fear, humiliation, shock, and depression are all types of emotional pain and suffering for which you may be compensated.

The usual basis for liability in personal injury is negligence. Negligence assigns liability based upon whether someone owes a duty of care to another person and whether that person breaches that duty by not meeting the required standard of conduct. The fact that you were injured, perhaps by another's unreasonable conduct, does not mean you are automatically entitled to compensation. You must prove the other person was negligent. Negligence is the failure of someone to exercise ordinary care to avoid injury to another's person or property. In order to prove someone's negligence was the cause of your injuries, you must prove the following elements: (1) the defendant owed a duty of care to you, (2) the defendant breached that duty, and (3) the defendants breach directly and proximately caused your injury. In a typical personal injury case, you are seeking compensation from the party-at-fault's insurance company. For example, if a driver of a vehicle is injured and goes to the emergency room because the driver of another vehicle swerved into the oncoming lane while texting, it could be argued that the texting-driver owed a duty of care to the plaintiff and caused damages when he or she breached that duty by texting while driving. All insurance companies employ attorneys whose sole purpose is to defend against these types of claims. This is why it is important to consult with an experienced personal injury attorney as soon as possible following an accident.

Strict liability is another basis for liability. It holds parties liable for injuries without proving any level of fault such as negligence. Strict liability is still widely used but occurs less frequently than negligence. Product manufacturers and designers are held strictly liable for injuries from defective products without a requirement that the plaintiff prove the manufacturer or designer's fault. In those types of cases, the plaintiff needs to show the product was defective and that the damages sustained were caused by the defective product. Other than strict liability for defective products, dog bite cases can sometimes impose strict liability upon the owner or keeper of a dog who bites someone. There is oftentimes no need to show the dog's owner was negligent (i.e. walking an untrained and aggressive dog in public while off a leash). Instead, the dog's owner or keeper could be liable simply for owning a dog that bit someone unprovoked. Lastly, activities that could be considered extremely dangerous, such as transporting ultrahazardous chemicals or handling explosives, might impose strict liability.

You may be asking yourself, when should you reach out to an attorney about a potential personal injury claim? The general rule is the sooner the better, and, as long as the statute of limitations for your claim has not lapsed, you can bring a claim. Depending on the type of claim you have, the statute of limitations sets a maximum time limit for when a claim can be brought. In most civil cases in Oklahoma, the statute of limitations is set at two years from the date of the accident or injury giving rise to the claim. However, there are certain instances in Oklahoma where the statute of limitations or the requirement to give notice of a claim can be as little as one year or possibly shorter.

CHAPTER 2

FIRST STEPS THAT I NEED TO TAKE TO GIVE MY CASE THE BEST POSSIBLE OUTCOME

What To Do After a Car Accident

When speaking to the police at the scene of an automobile accident, you should be honest, tell them your version of the events, let them know whether you are hurt, and tell them whether you were wearing a seatbelt. If you can think of any other cause of the wreck other than the other driver, then make sure to identify that with the police. If possible, you should take photographs of the scene of the accident, including the other person's vehicle, your vehicle, any debris on the street, any skid marks on the street, and the surrounding area (e.g. the intersection where the wreck occurred).

When you are speaking with the other party, be polite, but don't admit fault. Be advised that anything you say to the other party or the police officer could be used against you at a later time in your civil case. You should collect the other party's insurance information, as well as take a picture of their insurance card and driver's license. You should also collect the name, address, and phone number of anyone who claims to have witnessed the wreck or might have any important information or evidence. Believe it or not, police officers often omit witness contact information from their reports, so it is imperative that someone obtains it at the time of the wreck.

If your medical condition is such that you feel an ambulance ride to the hospital is necessary, then certainly take an ambulance. If you can go to the hospital on your own, then do so. Broken bones, significant pain, lightheadedness, heart palpations, tightness in your chest, and any other symptoms that concern you definitely warrant a trip to the emergency room. However, it is often the case that injury symptoms may not manifest themselves until a few hours or days after the wreck, when the adrenaline from the traumatic experience has dissipated. If you do not notice any injuries while at the scene of the wreck, tell the officer that you are unsure whether you have sustained an injury, as this will hopefully prompt the officer to note there is possible injury (rather than no injury).

Once you are being medically evaluated, make sure to be honest with the medical practitioners, identify the area of pain or injury, notify the doctor of any preexisting conditions, and ensure that your injuries are being documented. If you don't document your injuries, then the insurance adjusters and the lawyers working for them will say the injuries don't exist. After you've been released from the hospital, follow up with your primary care physician. In Oklahoma, some primary care physicians will not see a motor vehicle accident client because they're not set up to handle the billing aspect of the case. Under these circumstances, you should seek out specific facilities and medical practitioners that treat victims of automobile wrecks. An attorney in the area should be able to provide you with a list of providers who will treat you.

Don't let a gap in treatment arise because you think you'll get better. Insurance companies and defense attorneys will use a gap in treatment against you. The best advice is to follow the doctor's orders, go to all of your follow-up appointments, and identify every injury, even if it's not bothering you as severely as your other injuries. If the doctor recommends additional treatment or diagnostic testing (e.g. physical therapy, MRI, CT scan, injection), then follow those recommendations without delay.

In conclusion, seek medical treatment if you've been injured. Your health and well-being are of the utmost importance. Sometimes people don't notice symptoms of an injury immediately after the accident and start to feel it hours or days after. Some don't seek medical treatment immediately because they don't want to incur the expense of medical bills. However, if your injury is not adequately documented in medical records it will be very difficult for you to prove your claim even if you were injured.

Continue treatment and recommendations your provider(s) gives you. A significant gap in treatment can negatively affect your case.

What Is The Statute Of Limitations For A Personal Injury Case In Oklahoma?

The statute of limitations generally refers to the time limit on filing a lawsuit. The statute of limitations for a personal injury case in Oklahoma is usually two years from the date of the injury Certain cases such as those involving a governmental entity have a statute of limitations (or notice requirement) of one year. If the statute of limitations (or notice requirement) is missed, then you will be forever barred from making a claim. If you are unsure as to whether or not your case needs to be filed within a certain amount of time, I encourage you to contact an attorney immediately. You do not want to call a lawyer at the last minute; in fact, most lawyers will not take a case if they have fewer than two weeks to prepare and file it.

CHAPTER 3

FACTORS THAT MAKE A PERSONAL INJURY CASE VIABLE

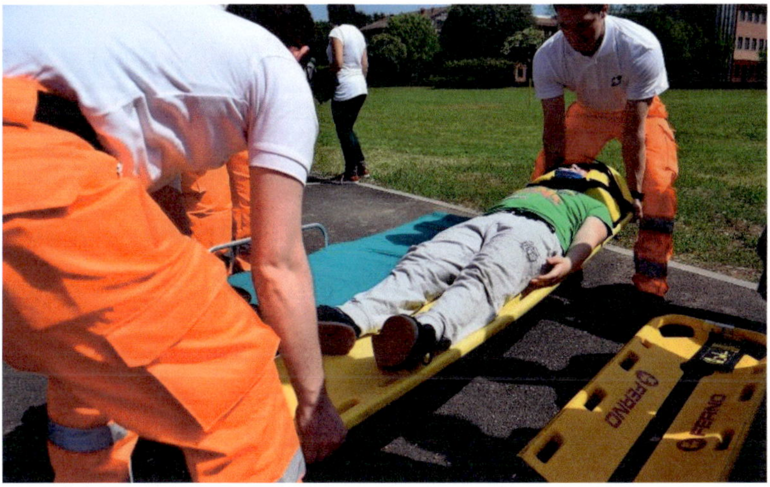

Just because you have been injured does not mean you will have a personal injury case. I was trained that in order to make a personal injury case you must have three legs of a stool: (1) liability, (2) damages, and (3) the ability to collect.

Liability: Someone else was negligent and caused your injuries.

Damages: Medical expenses, lost income, pain and suffering. There has to be damages. Just because someone did something wrong does not mean they have to pay you money. The wrongful act must cause damages.

Ability to Collect: This is the leg of the stool that causes plaintiffs, and plaintiff lawyers, the most heartache and difficulty. You may have a case where liability is clear, damages are significant but there is no insurance or any other way to collect money for your client. In other words, you can't get blood out of a turnip.

You must have all three legs of the stool for a personal injury case to be viable.

What Is A Hit-And-Run Case?

A hit and run is when someone causes a wreck and then leaves the scene of the wreck. It is illegal to leave the scene of a wreck. The first thing to determine when involved in a hit-and-run accident is whether the at-fault individual can be tracked down and held responsible. Next, we will determine whether there is uninsured or underinsured motorist coverage available.

Just because you have been involved in a hit-and-run does not necessarily mean that you don't have a case. It's still worth it to have a lawyer investigate the case, attempt to identify and locate the at-fault party, and seek alternative means of collecting for your injuries.

What If A Big Truck Was Involved In My Wreck?

Truckers are required by law to adhere to certain rules and regulations which don't apply to the general public. If a tractor-trailer is involved in your wreck it is extremely important to involve an attorney quickly so a proper investigation can be completed and evidence can be preserved. This will sometimes include using a wreck investigator who can go to the scene and document the evidence as well as attempt to download critical evidence and information from the tractor before it is destroyed.

Will My Preexisting Condition Preclude Me From Bringing A Viable Personal Injury Case?

Do not give up on your case just because you have a preexisting medical condition. Under Oklahoma law, you are allowed to recover for any aggravation of a preexisting medical condition. In fact, preexisting medical conditions sometimes better enable an attorney to explain to the jury the specific ways in which the client has been injured by the incident. For example, someone with a preexisting injury may be more susceptible to an injury from a particular wreck. Someone that has injured their neck prior to a wreck might be more prone to injury then someone with no prior injury.

What Compensation/ Damages Can I Seek In My Personal Injury Case?

When negotiating a settlement with the liable party, our goal is to have our clients compensated for *all* damages associated with their claim. This can include medical expenses, pain and suffering, loss of wages, punitive damages (if applicable), loss of consortium, future losses and future medical expenses. This will also vary case by case as some damages and injuries are worse than others.

How Is The Worth Of A Personal Injury Case Determined?

I get asked all the time "what is my case worth" or "how much will you be able to get me." These questions rely heavily on the extent of your damages. Any lawyer who promises you a certain amount of money for your case when you first meet is just blowing smoke and should be a red flag. I would suspect they are simply trying to convince you to hire them, and I would also suggest you run as fast as you can. Simply put, there is no way to establish what your case is worth until you have completed your medical treatment, identified all of your injuries and done an investigation; all of which take time. My standard response to questions relating to financial compensation and recovery is that I will work as hard as I can to get you all the money you are legally entitled to recover from the at-fault party. Once I have more knowledge as to your damages, liability, and other facts, I will be in a better position to estimate the value of your claim. I will usually provide a range of possible outcomes, understanding there is no way to accurately predict the exact value of your case. The only way to determine for sure what your case is worth is to ask 12 jurors to make that determination. Even then, two very similar cases can have drastically different values depending on the parties involved, facts of the case, and the injuries sustained.

How Are The Costs of Long-Term Care, Future Surgeries And Treatments Calculated In Serious Injury Cases?

We hire experts who are highly qualified to calculate future costs. Our experts analyze information from interviews, medical records, educational material, publications, studies, consultations with other professionals, medical providers and diagnostic evaluations to assess clients' abilities and needs. These experts are very good at using the information they gather and putting together a future life care plan or estimating future lost wages.

Chapter 4

How Does Comparative Negligence Affect A Personal Injury Case?

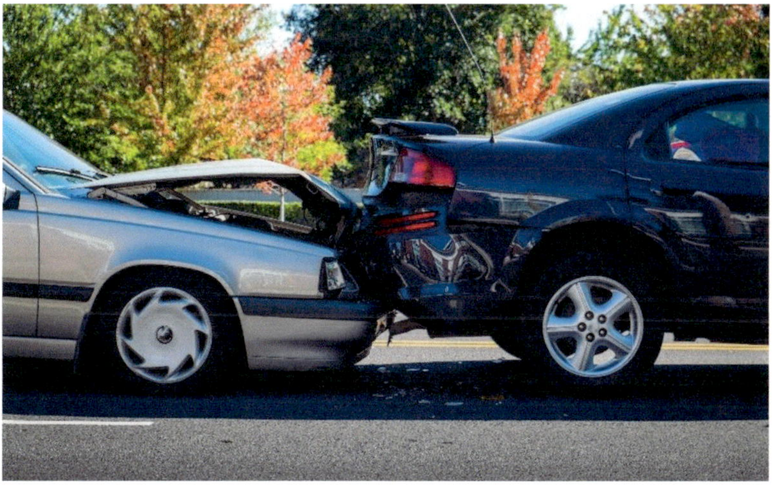

Comparative negligence is when the plaintiff is partially responsible for the incident that caused his or her injuries. This could reduce the compensation to which they are entitled if their negligent actions increased the probability of the accident. Insurance companies and defense attorneys will almost always attempt to establish comparative negligence and place a percentage of fault on the plaintiff.

Oklahoma is a comparative fault state, which means that the responsibility of each person in a car accident is assessed to determine fault based on each person's role in the accident. Each person's actions leading up to an accident will affect the amount of compensation they receive for their injuries.

Comparative negligence will not bar recovery unless the injured plaintiff's negligence is greater than the negligence of the defendant. 23 O.S. § 13. If a defendant argues the plaintiff was comparatively negligent then the defendant has the burden to prove that plaintiff contributed to the incident. Where contributory negligence is shown on the injured person's part, the amount of recovery will be reduced in proportion to the contributory negligence. 23 O.S. § 14. Oklahoma's Comparative Negligence rule allows the plaintiff to recover as long as he or she isn't determined to be more than 50% at fault. For example, the driver of a vehicle was injured in a vehicle collision where another vehicle's driver was determined to be 51% at fault and the injured plaintiff was determined to be 49% at fault. In a suit by the injured plaintiff against the other vehicle's driver, the plaintiff is permitted to recover 51% of the amount of damages because his or her total damages are reduced by 49%, which is his or her allocated share of negligence. A plaintiff generally benefits greatly from counsel by a personal injury attorney experienced at establishing the fault of a negligent party who caused the injuries. And, importantly, an experienced personal injury attorney will argue against any defense where the other side attempts to say that you, the injured plaintiff, caused or contributed to the incident.

Punitive Damages In Oklahoma

Some personal injury cases call for an award of punitive damages. Punitive damages are different from economic damages and non-economic damages in a couple ways. First, punitive damages aren't awarded to compensate the injured. They are awarded to punish the defendant's conduct and to discourage others from performing similar acts. Punitive damages are sometimes appropriate in personal injury cases where the jury is persuaded that the defendant has acted in reckless disregard for the rights of others or where the defendant has acted with malice. If the jury decides that the defendant did not act with malice or reckless disregard for the rights of others, then punitive damages will not be awarded. Reckless disregard describes conduct where the defendant was either aware, or did not care, that there was a substantial and unnecessary risk that his or her conduct would cause serious injury to others. Malice describes either hatred, spite, ill-will, or other intentional wrongful act without justification.

When the jury decides the defendant has acted with malice or reckless disregard for the rights of others, the next step is for the jury to determine the amount of the award. According to 23 O.S. § 9.1, in determining the amount, the jury can consider the following factors: (1) The seriousness of the hazard to the public arising from the defendant's misconduct; (2) The profitability of the misconduct to the defendant; (3) How long the conduct lasted and whether it is likely to continue; (4) Whether there were attempts to conceal the misconduct; (5) How aware the defendant was of the conduct and its consequences and how aware the defendant was of the hazard and of its excessiveness;

(6) The attitude and conduct of the defendant upon finding out about the misconduct/hazard; (7) The financial condition of the defendant; (8) The number and level of employees involved in causing or concealing the misconduct (if the defendant is a corporation or entity). Further, depending on whether the defendant's conduct is determined to be malicious or with reckless disregard for the rights of others, punitive damages can be capped at certain levels in Oklahoma. An experienced personal injury attorney will know how to analyze your situation and tell you whether punitive damages should be pursued.

Additional Considerations

A few years ago, the Oklahoma legislature passed a law that allows doctors, hospitals, physical therapists and other medical practitioners to file liens on cases. A lien looks like a nasty document that affects your house and makes most people mad when they receive them in the mail, but, ultimately, what it does is put everyone in the case—including the insurance company, defendant, you, and your lawyer—on notice that there is a third-party medical practitioner making a claim against the settlement proceeds. The lien does not affect your house, property, vehicle, or bank account.

The purpose behind this law is to enable medical practitioners to render medical services to potentially uninsured people with the expectation that they will get paid from the case. At some point, when the case resolves, attorneys will attempt to negotiate the lien. If you receive a lien in the mail, there is no need to stress about it because its what medical practitioners do in order to protect their interests for the services they render. If not for the lien statute, it would be difficult to find a medical practitioner willing to treat you as a result of an injury sustained in an accident.

CHAPTER 5

INSURANCE THAT MAY BE APPLICABLE IN OKLAHOMA

In Oklahoma, the minimum automobile liability coverage is 25/50/25, which means there is $25,000 available for any individual who is injured or killed in a wreck, and $50,000 total available for all people injured or killed, and finally, $25,000 available to pay property damage. For example, if two people were injured in a wreck, then there would be $50,000 in available coverage, but neither individual could receive more than $25,000.

In Oklahoma, there are many uninsured drivers, which is why I always tell people to get underinsured or uninsured motorist coverage. This type of coverage is inexpensive and will cover your bodily injury damages associated with an auto wreck related injury in the event that the at-fault party has insufficient insurance or no insurance at all. For example, if you sustain an injury that results in a $50,000 medical bill and the tortfeasor has only $25,000 in coverage, then your underinsured motorist coverage could potentially pay up to the limits of your policy.If you are injured by an uninsured driver your uninsured motorist coverage will be there to pay your damages. I tell everyone to buy as much under or uninsured motorist coverage as they can afford.

If you have an uninsured motorist policy, then it will likely apply to you regardless of whether you are in a vehicle that is covered by uninsured motorist coverage. The exception to this is if you are on a motorcycle at the time of a wreck. To elaborate, the Oklahoma Supreme Court has said that if you are in a wreck while on a motorcycle, the uninsured motorist policy that applies to one of your other vehicles will not pay for excess damages on your motorcycle. For this reason, your motorcycle coverage should include an uninsured or underinsured motorist policy.

There are several other forms of coverage in Oklahoma, such as an umbrella policy, which kick in once the policy limits of the bodily injury insurance coverage have been met. There is also comprehensive inclusion coverage, which applies to vehicle property damage. For example, if your vehicle was damaged due to a wreck for which you were at fault, then you would pay the deductible on your policy in order to have your vehicle repaired. Rental insurance would pay for a rental car while your vehicle is being repaired.

Medical payments coverage (MedPay) covers medical expenses incurred by those who were involved in the wreck. I highly recommend you get as much of this coverage as possible, because it should pay the medical bills associated with your wreck. Passengers who were in your vehicle at the time of a wreck have a right to make a claim against your underinsured or uninsured motorist policy as well as your MedPay policy. As it relates to a passenger, MedPay may be subject to subrogation, meaning that once the passenger receives a third-party settlement, they might have to pay back the money they collected from MedPay.

In Oklahoma, rideshare companies, such as Uber and Lyft, are required to have an insurance policy that covers their drivers. In addition, Uber and Lyft drivers are required to have personal coverage on their vehicle. This personal coverage might not pay for damages that are sustained while an Uber or Lyft driver is on the clock and in the process of transporting people. This is because many of these drivers have a regular insurance policy rather than a commercial policy, and regular insurance policies contain an exclusion that applies when the driver is charging a fare. Although the coverage on the automobile itself may be denied based on that exclusion, the rideshare company is required to maintain a policy that provides coverage under these circumstances to the passengers.

When buying automobile insurance, you may wonder how much is enough. Uninsured/underinsured motorist coverage and MedPay policies are there to protect you, the people in your vehicle, and your family members, so you should buy as much of that coverage as you can afford. If you can afford it, I also recommend buying comprehensive and collision, rental insurance, and an umbrella policy.

What's The Difference Between Paid Expenses And Incurred Expenses?

About five years ago, the Oklahoma Legislature passed a tort reform bill that altered the way attorneys are allowed to present medical evidence to a jury. This statute is written in a very complicated manner and creates confusion to many who are not familiar with the way it works. In the past, attorneys were able to show the total billed amount of medical expenses to the jury. Due to this bill, we can now only present the amount of paid medical expenses. This usually reduces the amount of damages a jury will award an injured person. Since the amounts paid are normally significantly less than the amount charged, then verdicts are usually correspondingly lower. Plaintiffs run the risk of a jury thinking that since the medical expense is so low then they must not have been hurt too bad. Even more important is the fact that a low number may anchor a jury and psychologically push them to a lower verdict amount. To explain further, if you have health insurance and it paid your bills, we only get to show the jury the amount that was paid by your health insurance policy, as well as copays and deductibles. For example, if your emergency room bill was $10,000, your copay was $100, your deductible was $100, and the health insurance policy covered $300, then instead of being able to show the jury that the bill was $10,000, we would only able to show that it was $500. There are certain limitations, restrictions, and exceptions to this rule, but generally speaking the paid amount of your medical expense is what a jury will see. Under some circumstances, bills that are not paid by health insurance, as well as medical liens can be shown to the jury. The insurance companies and defense attorneys will go to great lengths to attempt to get your medical bills reduced. They do this in an attempt to minimize the medical bills as well as anchor a jury. They believe the lower the bills they present to a jury, the more likely it will be that a jury will minimize your injury or not believe you were hurt as bad as you claim. They think if a jury sees someone with small medical bills then they must not have been hurt too badly. Just remember medical bills for a broken arm can be significantly less than medical bills for a strained back. Both are serious injuries and cause differing types of pain and lasting symptoms. I believe that bills have no correlation to the type of injury you sustained, how badly you were hurt or the extent of your damages. Sometimes we will even waive medical bills in front of a jury so that we can direct the jury's focus away from the bills, a small number that has no bearing on what you have gone through, towards the actual injury you sustained.

CHAPTER 6

WILL THE INSURANCE COMPANY HAVE ACCESS TO MY PAST AND PRESENT MEDICAL HISTORY?

In short, yes. With respect to all body parts you declare injured in an accident, the opposing attorney will ask whether you have ever injured or suffered any ailment, pains, disease or sickness to that body part before or after the accident. They will then want to know the dates of the injuries and which healthcare providers saw you for those issues.

What Is My Responsibility, If Any, In Notifying My And The At Fault Party's Insurance Of The Incident And My Injury?

In regard to this question, contact an attorney as soon as possible. However, if no attorney is retained, it's best you contact both insurance companies as soon as possible to inform them of the incident and your damages, and start the process for your personal injury and property damage claim. The sooner the better.

What If The Other Party's Insurance Company Contacts Me? Should I Ever Give A Statement?

Do not give them a statement and tell them to contact your attorney for any information they're seeking. Whenever you retain an attorney they will send a letter of representation to the insurance company to inform them they've been hired to handle your claim and to direct any future contact and correspondence to their office. Insurance companies know not to contact you if they know you've hired legal representation. You are not required to give a statement to the other party's insurance company. Usually when the other side's insurance representative asks me for a statement of my client I will ask them to let me take a statement of their insured and the conversation stops there. However, sometimes I will allow a statement. For example, if it is a situation where I think a statement will help us or better explain damages I will agree to allow my client to give a statement. However, those situations are rare. Insurance representatives are specially trained to record your conversations to use against you later in your claim process. You could potentially hurt your case without knowing you are doing it.

Picking The Right Lawyer

Picking the right lawyer is very important. I would suggest you pick an attorney that you are comfortable will give you the amount of communication you desire and is skilled in the particular area of law in which you are seeking representation. You will likely be working with the attorney you pick for a considerable amount of time. You must be confident the attorney is honest, trustworthy, accessible, and competent in the area of law. Consult with an attorney to get legal advice as soon as possible. The attorney will review the factors of your claim to determine if you have a viable case against the at-fault party. At the consult, you can determine if you want to hire the attorney or not. If you are not comfortable with the attorney, seek another opinion or consultation with a different attorney.

Once you hire an attorney, provide the attorney with all information that could be relevant to your case and keep your attorney updated and informed with any relevant information that can be helpful. This includes informing them of all medical providers you've seen as a result of the injuries you sustained in the incident, notifying of any address and phone number changes, being available and compliant, keeping records of any documents you receive, not posting on social media, and always being honest. Lastly, be sure to inform your attorney if you move or change contact information.

CHAPTER 7

INSURANCE AND DEFENSE ATTORNEYS' STRATEGIES TO AVOID PAYING CLIENTS

Insurance companies and defense attorneys will do anything they can to point the finger at you or a third party in order to minimize their exposure or liability. For example, they might blame you of faking or malingering, try to convince the jury that your injuries were pre-existing rather than caused by the incident in question, or even argue that an intervening event such as a fall or another auto wreck caused your injuries.

Another tactic used by defense attorneys and insurance companies is to delay cases with the goal of pushing you to the point where you simply give up and do whatever necessary to end the case. Defense attorneys bill by the hour. That being said, they will find any reason to drag out litigation. Remember, the longer a case lasts the more money defense attorneys will make.

Another strategy employed by insurance companies and defense attorneys is to attack you personally and paint you in a negative light. They might also use the defense medical examination as a way to poke holes in your case or use your past medical history against you. Often, the defense can rely upon these hired doctors to provide a medical opinion that minimizes your injuries or need for future treatment. It is your lawyer's job to cross-examine these paid defense experts and build an arsenal against them. However, these defense doctors are trained expert witnesses and they often do a good job of minimizing or destroying a plaintiff's case.

Another technique used by insurance companies and defense attorneys is called an offer to confess judgment. There are a couple of different mechanisms by which they use this, which are set out in Oklahoma Statutes. Ultimately, the defense attorney may file an offer to confess judgement whereby they offer a certain amount of money and you have a certain amount of time to accept their offer. An offer to confess judgment must be accepted within a certain time period. If the time period lapses without an acceptance, or if you deny or decline that offer and do not get a better verdict at trial, then you could potentially be on the hook for the other side's attorney fees and costs, or a portion thereof. In essence, the offer to confess is just another arrow in their quiver to shoot at you in order to pressure you into an unreasonable settlement.

CHAPTER 8

HOW DO YOU DECIDE WHETHER OR NOT TO SETTLE A PERSONAL INJURY CASE?

There are multiple reasons why it is a good idea to settle a personal injury case. If I have a client who, I am confident, will not make a good witness, or one who does not want to file a lawsuit, or a client who has a background that could negatively impact their case, then I might advise them against pursuing a lawsuit. However, if I have a good client with a good case with enough damages to justify a lawsuit, I may suggest proceeding with a lawsuit or trial. In each case, I review the estimated costs of a lawsuit and trial, as well as the risks associated with pursuing a lawsuit or going to trial with my client. As my client, I want you to know the good, the bad, and the ugly regarding litigation and trial. Defense attorneys and insurance carriers are trained to dig into your past and bring up things that are absolutely not relevant to the case—things that embarrass you and paint you in a bad light before a jury. I believe that one of the most important requirements of going to trial is to make sure that the client is a good and likeable person. If a jury does not like a plaintiff then it is very hard to convince a jury to help a client.

In evaluating a case for potential litigation, we also want to decide whether there is a 'mad' factor, which means any reason a jury might get angry. For example, it's unlikely that a jury would be mad at a 70-year- old church-going grandmother of 10 who simply made a mistake and bumped the rear end of a vehicle. It's a lot more likely that a jury would be upset at a driver who caused a wreck as a result of using methamphetamine. If a jury gets mad, they are more likely to render a significant verdict for the claimant. If a jury doesn't have a reason to be angry or simply thinks the defendant made a mistake then the jury is more likely to minimize the damages they award you.

After evaluating a settlement offer and analyzing the probable outcome of the case, we will decide whether to pursue litigation. If your case is worth $15,000, the insurance company has offered $10,000, and it will cost $10,000 to litigate your case, then I will likely tell you that it isn't economical to litigate your case. We must consider the merits and value of the case in order to justify the time, expense, and risk of trial. Although many cases do not end up in a trial, it is important to note we prepare every case as if it will end up going to trial from the very beginning.

How Are Settlement Funds Disbursed?

Once we resolve your case, it may take weeks (or in some situations months) in order to collect the money. Once money is collected, it will be deposited into our trust account to allow the bank to collect the funds. During that time, we will negotiate medical expenses. In addition, attorney fees, costs, medical liens, certain health insurance payments, expenses you direct us to pay, and any other expense that's associated with your claim that by contract you owe, will be paid for from the settlement amount. The remaining balance will be paid to you.

You are required to pay medical liens and certain amounts some health insurance companies pay. There are some situations where you may choose to not pay certain medical expense. Should you choose to not pay some of the medical bills with your settlement money, you would still be legally responsible for paying the remaining amount at some point should the providers attempt to collect on the bills. Some clients choose to pay for the medical expenses as they arise or as the medical provider attempts to collect payment, because at that point, they may be better able to negotiate the amount the medical provider will accept as full and final payment.

CHAPTER 9

WHAT FACTORS MAY CAUSE MY PERSONAL INJURY CASE TO GO TO LITIGATION?

Insurance adjusters are trained to look for ways to not pay you, and they will dispute liability even when liability is clear. They will try to blame you for the wreck or the injury, and do anything they can to move the focus away from any evidence of negligence or recklessness on behalf of their insured. Cases that do go to litigation usually involve disputes over liability or disputes regarding the reasonableness and/or necessity of medical treatment. With that said, we may take a case to trial simply because we believe the case is worth significantly more than what's being offered by the insurance company.

Although we cannot predict with 100 percent certainty what the jury will decide, we can come up with a probable outcome based on our education and experience in the field over the past 18 years. We keep track of every verdict in the state of Oklahoma in order to evaluate cases for litigation. Certainly, there are never any guarantees and a jury can award more or less than what we expect. The choice to proceed to trial will always be that of the client. Our job is to provide all of the available information to you so you can make an educated choice about whether or not to go to trial.

What Can I Expect If My Case Goes To Litigation?

Once we decide to proceed with litigation, we will draft a lawsuit wherein we outline the facts and allegations of the case. If it is filed in federal court, it is called a complaint. If it's filed in state court, it is called a petition. Once the case has been assigned to a specific judge, we will issue summons and serve the lawsuit upon the defendants. In most cases, a defendant is given 20 days to respond with an answer to the complaint or petition. In the answer, the defendant will either admit or deny our allegation in the petition. This will frame the issues that will be litigated. If the defendant admits to the allegations, then litigation won't be necessary to prove those allegations. If the defendant denies the allegations, then the issues will need to be litigated.

At this point, the discovery phase of litigation begins. We will send written discovery (i.e. interrogatories, requests for production of documents and requests for admissions) to the other side, and vice versa. We will properly respond to the questions and produce the discoverable documents. The discovery phase is broad, and, in general, the other side can request many things that may or may not be used at trial. We may also send subpoenas and use other discovery mechanisms to gather additional information. It might be appropriate to conduct background checks on witnesses or defendants, or send private investigators to speak with witnesses.

The next step in the process is to conduct oral depositions, which we generally do on the defendant unless the defendant has already admitted liability. We also present our client for deposition and possibly take depositions of other witnesses. During this stage in the process, we likely file a motion to enter, which essentially informs the court that we believe the case is ready to be set on the trial docket. While this does not necessarily mean the case is going to trial, it gives us the ability to set deadlines. This is important, because many cases don't get settled unless there are deadlines. Nothing settles cases better than a looming trial date. We will appear in front of the judge, who will enter a scheduling order. This scheduling order sets the case for pretrial and sets deadlines for discovery, witness and exhibit lists, experts, medical examinations, and other deadlines that are necessary to keep the case moving toward a resolution.

The defense is entitled to have the plaintiff examined by a doctor of their choosing at what they like to call an "independent medical examination." The proper term for this examination is "defense medical examination" because the doctors who perform them are not independent at all. They are hired and paid by the insurance company and defense attorneys. In essence, they are hired and trained to defeat or minimize the plaintiff's case. During the defense medical examination, the most important thing to do is answer questions truthfully and accurately. We will sometimes video these medical examinations just to make sure the doctor does not misrepresent what occurred during the exam.

There may or may not be a deadline to mediate the case. We may be ordered or we may simply agree to mediate your case. Generally speaking, mediation is beneficial in that it helps settle most cases and it allows us to identify weaknesses and strengths in the case that otherwise might go undetected. We cannot properly evaluate a case until we understand where the possible weaknesses lie. If mediation is pursued, we decide (in conjunction with the other side) who should act as the third-party mediator. Mediation can last anywhere from 10 minutes to two days, or even longer. During mediation, it is our hope we can convince the defense attorney or insurance carrier to offer the most they're willing to pay to settle the case without going to trial.

At that point, the lawyer goes through the same process they did before the case was filed (i.e. estimate the cost of taking the case to trial, discuss the risks and probable outcomes of the case and run the numbers) so the plaintiff can make a good, sound, unemotional business decision about whether or not to settle the case or proceed to trial. If the case doesn't settle at mediation, it may still settle prior to trial. However, we will continue preparations for trial, which will include lining up doctors, getting the witnesses ready, and preparing our exhibits. This is when the case can become very expensive, which is why we try to first resolve it through mediation.

The length of time before the actual trial will occur depends on the county where it's being held. For example, in Oklahoma County, most trial dates are being scheduled four to six months from the time we request one. In other jurisdictions, we may have to wait years for a trial date. During the litigation process, we prepare to present the case in the best light and advocate for as much money as we can legally and ethically obtain. It should be noted that just because a case has been set for trial does not mean that the trial will actually occur. By simply preparing for trial, it will likely cause the insurance carrier, defense attorneys, and defendants to avoid it by paying what is necessary to resolve the case.

Does The Threat Of Going To Trial Enhance The Likelihood Of A Larger Settlement From An Insurance Company?

Insurance companies and defense attorneys know which lawyers will try a lawsuit. They watch every verdict that comes out of the state of Oklahoma. It will add significant value to your case to hire a lawyer who has a reputation of taking cases to trial when necessary. Most lawyers are scared to go to the courthouse and try a lawsuit, or, they are simply too lazy. This is why you should look for a lawyer who has a history of trial experience. It is a good idea to ask a lawyer how many cases they have tried to a jury over the last 12-24 months.

Going to trial can be a risk for both parties. The plaintiff risks being compensated less than what they were initially offered or receiving zero while the defendant risks being required to pay more than what they offered. Should the case go to trial, the jurors are the ones who will decide how much the claim is worth.

How Does Going To Trial Affect The Overall Costs?

Going to trial is very expensive. On a regular run-of-the-mill case, we spend about $10,000 to $20,000 in litigation expenses. If we decide to take a case to trial, we will spend the money that is necessary to get it ready for trial. That does not mean we will spend unnecessary amounts or that we will spend money on everything. This means the closer you get to trial, the costlier it becomes, and ultimately that is money coming out of your pocket. However, being prepared and showing the defense attorneys that you mean business and are ready for trial adds value to your case.

How Does Going To Trial Affect The Overall Costs Of The Personal Injury Process And My Settlement?

Why is going to trial costly? There are many expenses incurred in prepping for trial such as hiring experts, paying doctors for their time, purchasing materials to support your claim, etc. Plaintiff attorneys usually work on contingency fee contracts, meaning they get a percentage of the plaintiff's settlement and get any case expenses reimbursed. If the case is lost and no settlement was recovered, the client usually doesn't owe the attorney anything, sometimes not even the costs incurred. Because the cost of going to trial is expensive, I as a plaintiff attorney run the risk of losing thousands of dollars. Ultimately, if there is a settlement, the attorney will be reimbursed for the costs he funded.

After the motion to enter, there are pretrial motions. This is the point where the parties may file discovery motions, motions to compel, or a motion for summary judgment. Based on an issue of liability or technicality, the defendant may ask the court to dismiss the entire case. There will also be trial motions prior to trial, which include motions in limine and Daubert challenges, whereby both sides may ask the court to limit expert opinions or strike experts. The average length of trial for a typical run-of-the-mill car wreck case is two or three days. For a complex medical malpractice case, it could take two weeks to try the case. Once a verdict is rendered, you will be faced with post-trial motions, such as motions for new trial or motions to set aside or reduce the verdict. In addition, you will face the potential of an appeal.

What Happens After The Trial?

There are many things that can happen after a trial, including post-trial motions, potential motions for attorney fees, motions for costs, motions for a new trial, and motions for remittitur. Even if you lose the case, there's still a chance that the case will resolve depending on whether or not there is potential reversible error at the trial. If an appeal occurs, it likely takes one to two years before a decision on the appeal is rendered. It is important to note that the costs of an appeal can be very significant.

CHAPTER 10

COMMON MISTAKES PEOPLE MAKE IN A PERSONAL INJURY CLAIM

Waiting to hire a lawyer is a common mistake. The longer you wait, the more likely it is that witnesses will be impossible to contact and evidence will be lost or destroyed. In addition, the closer you are to the statute of limitations, the more difficult it will be to find a lawyer who will agree to take your case. Another common mistake is to allow gaps in medical treatment by missing appointments or not following through with referrals. The insurance company and defense attorney will argue that gaps in treatment indicate you weren't actually injured or in pain.

It is also a big mistake to not identify or describe your injuries to medical providers. Often times, people will only identify the injury causing them the most pain. The problem with this is that what seems like a minor injury can develop into something more serious over time. If this happens and there was never any mention of the injury in the medical records, then it will be very difficult to recover for that injury.

It is critical to be consistent with your story at all times. Inconsistent statements kill cases. Inconsistency can arise when people intentionally lie or deceive, when they get confused, or simply make a mistake when recounting what occurred. As long as you are truthful, you have nothing to worry about.

You should never exaggerate your injuries, because this can reduce your credibility in the eyes of a jury. For example, if you were to say that on a pain scale of 1 to 10 your pain is at a 12, that might not be believable unless something catastrophic has just happened to you.

The mere fact you are talking, walking, able to feed yourself, and able to answer questions would cast doubt on a pain rating that's quite literally off the charts.

Problems can also arise by posting comments or photos about your injury or the incident on social media. The insurance carriers and defense attorneys will use even the most innocent post against you at trial. As an example, I once represented a lovely college student who had a case with clear liability. She was offered a decent settlement, but I felt the case was worth more so the client and I decided we would not accept the settlement and, instead go to trial. At trial, the number one exhibit the defense used was photographs taken from my client's social media page showing her wearing high heels in a costume on Halloween (approximately 6 weeks after the wreck). The jury ultimately found in our favor, but the award was much lower than what I'd hoped. When interviewing the jurors afterward, they said the reason they didn't award more money was because of the picture: since she was wearing high heels, in a costume, at a party, having fun a month and a half after the wreck, they assumed she wasn't as injured as she claimed.

Another common mistake is to borrow money against your case. If you find yourself in a position where you need money, reach out to friends or family members. I always advise against using a company that offers to loan you the money against your case. Why? Because these companies charge exorbitant fees and interest, which will make your case almost impossible to settle. Don't borrow money on your case unless you absolutely have to, and only do that once you have exhausted all other resources.

Changing lawyers during a case is also a mistake. In fact, one of the biggest red flags is when a client has already worked with two or more attorneys on the same case. This usually indicates that there is a problem with the client, or with the case itself. Choose a lawyer wisely from the beginning, and stick with that lawyer. If you feel like the lawyer is not communicating with you, call them or schedule a meeting with them. Do not change lawyers unless you absolutely have to, because it will hurt your case and affect the way defense attorneys and insurance companies view your case.

Chapter 11

Do I Really Need A Lawyer?

Whether you need to hire a lawyer or not depends in large part upon the type of case you have. However, if you are asking yourself whether or not you should hire a lawyer, then the answer is probably yes. If you have a premises liability case, significant damage case, or complex liability case, I would advise you to hire a lawyer. Trucking, aviation, and environmental cases are complex and should always be handled by an attorney. In contrast, a run-of-the-mill soft tissue injury case might not require you to hire an attorney, but doing so would certainly add value to your case. A lawyer is trained to identify the strengths and weaknesses of your case, as well as deal with defense lawyers and insurance adjusters. Anything you say to an insurance representative or defense attorney will be twisted and used against you, so it's best to have an attorney speak on your behalf.

Hiring an attorney to handle your personal injury case comes with a number of benefits, including the following:

- You won't have to worry about handling the claims process, which includes collecting your records, talking to insurance adjusters, and negotiating your case.
- You will know your case is being handled properly.
- You will be able to focus on your health and well being.
- You will likely end up with a larger settlement than you would get on your own.

If you are wondering whether you should hire an attorney, I would suggest you at least talk to one and determine whether the services being offered justify the costs. Generally, a lawyer who handles personal injury litigation will work on a contingency fee basis, which means they will only get paid once they have helped you obtain a recovery. More importantly, they should not charge you for your initial consultation.

How Much Will A Lawyer Cost?

Typical personal injury cases usually cost 1/3 to 50 percent of the gross recovery, depending, on who you hire and what work was required. A complex medical negligence, aviation, or product liability case may cost closer to 50 percent of the gross recovery from the outset. We typically work on a sliding scale. Meaning that the percentage goes up depending on what stage in the process we are in when the case resolves. At no time will we ever charge more than 50 percent for attorney fees. Most lawyers will offer a free initial consultation so you can get your questions answered and decide whether you want to hire that lawyer. When you're looking for or interviewing lawyers, always think about the long-term relationship you will have with that person. If you do not like your lawyer or you are not comfortable with the lawyer you are interviewing, then that is not the right attorney for you. There may be times when you don't hear from the lawyer for extended periods of time, and you must be comfortable enough to have faith that the lawyer is properly working on the case and pushing it toward a successful resolution. Look for a lawyer who is honest, hardworking, and experienced in handling cases similar to yours.

What Do You Say To Potential Clients Who Are Maybe Thinking, "Liability Is Clear. I Can Handle This On My Own."?

If a potential client wants to handle a matter on their own I always tell them that that is fine and that they can call us anytime they may have questions. I will never push a person to hire our firm. However, mistakes can be made while dealing with the insurance company and many times they will try to use your own words against you. Once a mistake has been made, it is impossible to take it back. Insurance companies try to discount certain injuries and offer clients unreasonable settlements. This is why I believe it is important to hire an experienced professional who knows how the system works as soon as possible.

What Information Is Critical To Share With My Attorney Right From The Start?

It is important you share as much detailed information from the incident as you can. Provide any documentation you may have, such as insurance verifications, police reports, pictures, medical records and bills, etc. It is important you inform your attorney of the injuries you sustained and your treatment plan. Be sure to tell your attorney about any pre-existing medical issues so that they can be addressed from the beginning of your case. Insurance companies and defense attorneys will look at your past medical history to determine if your injuries are a result of the accident or if they are old injuries. That is not to say the incident didn't make your old injuries worse. As a plaintiff's attorney, we hire experts who can substantiate the cause of your current injuries.

CHAPTER 12

IF I HIRE JOE CARSON TO BE MY LAWYER, WHAT HAPPENS NEXT?

During an initial consultation, we will discuss all the details of your case, so you should come prepared with all of the information pertinent to the event (e.g. medical records, incident reports, accident reports, photographs, insurance information, etc.). After a thorough review of this information, I will decide whether I believe you have a case I can help resolve. If so, the next step would be to retain us (in Oklahoma, an attorney must receive a retainer agreement executed by the client prior to working on a case). If you decide to retain us, we will provide you with medical authorizations and other documents necessary to get your case started. Once those documents are executed, we will begin working on your case.

My office will open a file, give notice to the proper parties (including the defendant and insurance companies) and start gathering evidence. Some cases will require us to hire investigators, reconstructionist, or experts. While we do what's necessary to properly investigate the case, you will focus on getting better. If we need you, we will email, text, or call you. Should you have any questions, you can call our firm at any time or schedule an appointment to come in and see us.

Once a doctor has determined you have reached maximum medical improvement, meaning that further treatment will not improve your condition or your injuries have resolved, we will finalize the gathering of the medical records, medical bills, and other necessary documents in order to submit your claim to the insurance company. It is my belief we should usually submit a case for settlement before a lawsuit is filed in order to give the insurance company the opportunity to do what's right and settle the case. It usually takes about 60 to 90 days for an insurance company to review and make an offer on a run-of-the-mill case.

Once an offer is made, we will discuss it with you and decide how to proceed in order to make you as whole as possible. Once the negotiation process starts, we will go back and forth with the insurance company by email, letter, or telephone until we receive the highest amount they are willing to offer. Some insurance representatives are fair and reasonable, while others are not. We will discuss the pros and cons, as well as potential outcomes of accepting the offer versus proceeding with a lawsuit. I never tell clients what they should do. I simply give them all of the information they need in order to make an informed unemotional business decision that is right for them.

What Is It That Sets You Apart In Handling Serious Injury Cases?

Our mission at Warhawk Legal is to fight for justice by delivering exceptional legal representation to our clients through providing the highest quality guidance and support. We are a tenacious team dedicated to legal excellence in achieving outstanding results. We take pride in our commitment to delivering personalized solutions with a focus on our clients, communication and accessibility.

I believe that what sets me apart is Integrity, Strong Work Ethic, and Reputation. These are the cornerstones of practice at Warhawk Legal. In the legal profession, you only have your reputation. I say what I do and do what I say. There is no lawyer that will outwork me. The insurance companies and defense attorneys know I will try a case when needed. If your case needs to be tried by a jury, you can expect me to do that. In my 18 years of practice, I have built a network of connections and an honorable reputation that can be beneficial to my clients in helping to achieve the highest and best result on their cases.

CHAPTER 14

FREQUENTLY ASKED QUESTIONS

Q: If I Have Been Injured Does That Mean I Am Entitled To Receive Money?

Because you have been injured does not mean you automatically receive money damages. What you do have the right to do is (1) make a claim and (2) have an opportunity to prove by admissible evidence the incident was caused by the negligence of others and that the negligence was the direct cause of the injuries and damages you sustained.

Q: When Should I Hire A Lawyer After A Car Wreck?

For "fender benders" and routine car accident claims with no personal injuries, you may not need to hire a lawyer. However, if you have been injured, you should hire an attorney immediately.

Here are a few things to think about before deciding whether or not you should try to handle your own claim:

1: Is Fault Contested In Your Case Or Does The Other Driver And Insurance Company Admit Fault?

If there is a dispute over who caused the accident and you cannot prove the other driver is at fault, it may be best to retain an attorney. The stakes could be high and you could recover nothing.

2: How Much Are Your Out-Of-Pocket Expenses For Medical Bills And Lost Wages?

You must decide at what point your case is too big to handle yourself and when it is time to hire a lawyer.

3: How Badly Were You Injured And How Long Did It Take You To Recover?

If you have a serious injury or one that is permanent, you have a potentially large claim and should hire a lawyer who can present it in a professional manner.

4: Are You Going To Court?

If you are unable to resolve the situation outside of court, it is a good idea to hire a lawyer who knows the rules, can protect your legal rights, and give you a fighting chance at winning.

5: How Much Time Do You Want To Devote To The Case?

These types of cases can be confusing, time consuming, and costly. You are better off spending your time doing something you like to do or earning a living and letting someone else that handles these types of cases worry about your case.

Q: How Long Should I Wait Before Contacting A Lawyer?

The sooner a lawyer can get started working for you the better. Remember, in almost every situation when you are injured or have property damage, you have only a certain amount of time to file a claim. The longer you wait, the more difficult it may be to obtain the evidence you need to support your case. Furthermore, if you have submitted your claim to an insurance company, the insurance adjuster you are dealing with may have settled hundreds of cases in the past year alone. He or she is highly trained at negotiation. It is important to be very cautious in talking with an insurance adjuster; they are trained to save the insurance company money. If they can beat your case, they will try. They will use your own words against you. Be careful what you say to the trained professionals.

Q: What Documentation Should I Bring When I Meet With A Lawyer?

The more information you can provide, the easier it will be for an attorney to determine if your claim will be successful. You should supply any documents that may have a bearing on your case. Be overly prepared when deciding what to bring to your initial meeting with your attorney. While the documents you need to bring depends on the nature of the case, it is generally a good idea to bring any papers relating to the incident or the parties involved. Lawsuit papers, incident reports, photographs, medical records, medical bills, written statements, repair estimates, and invoices are all examples of items that may be important to your case, and will need to be shown to your lawyer. Information about the other driver's insurance is extremely helpful. It is also a prudent idea to bring a list of the names and contact information of anyone involved with the incident as well as all witness information. Prior to the first meeting, doing a timeline of important events relating to the incident can be helpful in terms of jogging your memory and assisting the attorney in understanding when and how things occurred. Remember, it's better to be over prepared than under prepared. If you haven't collected any documents prior to meeting with a lawyer, do not worry. The lawyer will be able to direct you in the right direction in obtaining the documents you may need.

Q: What Can I Expect At The Initial Consultation?

You will be asked to complete some simple intake forms much like going to a doctor's office. Most of the time the lawyer should be able to tell you whether you have a legal claim that has merit. If it does, you should discuss the terms of the lawyer's representation. If you have decided to choose that particular lawyer, he or she may ask you to sign a retainer agreement. A lawyer cannot represent you without a written retainer agreement. Once that agreement has been signed, your attorney will then start gathering information he or she will need to try your case. No competent lawyer should tell you what your case is worth at the first visit. To arrive at a figure for damages, your lawyer will need to examine the extent of your injuries, your pain and suffering, disability, disfigurement, the cost of medical treatment, and lost wages.

Q: What Are The Benefits Of Hiring A Lawyer?

Unfortunately, car accidents happen every day. Many of them result in minor vehicle damage and can generally be handled alone by contacting the insurance company. However, car accidents involving physical injury, fatality, or other significant damage may warrant the legal representation of an experienced personal injury accident attorney. Many times, in these types of serious accidents, you can sustain injuries that don't manifest themselves until later. If you settle with your insurance company, you may realize in the future that what you settled for didn't properly consider future complications. While certain matters, such as a minor fender bender, may not require an attorney's help, there are many instances where retaining an attorney would be beneficial to your case. First of all, a lawyer is able to navigate the complexities of the law as well as the legal jargon that may stump you and cause you to misinterpret the situation thereby hindering your case. Having a lawyer on your side can help you avoid problems, as opposed to fixing them once they arise. Money is most always a consideration for potential clients, so it is important to note that hiring an attorney can actually save you money. In fact, most lawyers provide a free initial consultation and many civil lawyers do not collect a dime unless they win your case. Remember an experienced lawyer has probably seen cases similar to yours or at least knows enough to make an educated guess about how it might resolve. Sometimes a settlement is the best choice and an attorney can help you fairly negotiate with the opposing party. Most importantly, a lawyer should be able to take some of the burden and stress of handling a case from you and will ensure your case is properly handled.

Q: What Will You Do For Me If I Hire You?

Our firm will make every effort to settle your claim without the necessity of litigation. Initially, we will notify the person or entity that may be at fault, as well as their insurance company. At that time, we will begin investigating the claim and preparing it to submit to the insurance companies. The insurance companies will also be investigating the claim. During this time, we may ask for periodic medical reports so we can follow the progress of your medical treatment. You may also be asked to give a statement to us, an insurance adjuster, or an attorney for the insurance company concerning the facts surrounding your claim. An attorney with our firm will be with you if you are required to give a statement, and we will explain this to you in further detail if your statement is necessary.

Q: How Long Will My Case Take?

BE PATIENT. The legal process has a pace of its own and cannot be hurried. Your case will not be submitted for settlement until it is ready for settlement. That does not mean that we will not be doing anything. In fact, we will be getting it ready to submit. Cases like yours are many times affected by events outside the control of any attorney. Possible delays in resolution of your case are too many to list but include things such as delayed medical treatment, failure of a client in communicating with the attorney, sickness of a party or adjuster, judge being out of town, and failure of an insurance company to conduct a meaningful and timely investigation. The more complex your case, the longer it will likely take to get it resolved. We want to get your case resolved as soon as possible and will pursue your claim with diligence. Generally, it is our desire to move your case as quickly as possible. However, sometimes the wisest course is not always the fastest. Remember, we don't get paid until you get paid.

Q: How Do I Pay A Lawyer On My Car Wreck Case?

When you hire our firm for your car or truck wreck, you will pay for the attorney fees only if you recover funds for your injuries. This is called a contingency fee agreement. The percentage paid to the attorney will differ based on the type of case, as well as the complexity of the case and the probability of success. For example, for a complex and/or difficult case, the attorney might charge 50% while for a simple car wreck case, the attorney might only charge 1/3 of the recovery.

It is important to note that costs are different than fees. For example, when you hire our firm, we will incur costs associated with your case. We will have to pay for things such as filing fees, medical records and police reports, as well as postage, copies, experts, investigators, etc. Every firm treats costs differently. We will usually front most costs and be paid back at the time of settlement from the client's portion of the settlement.

Q: If I Hire A Lawyer Does That Mean I Have To Go To Trial?

Not necessarily. The majority of cases resolve themselves prior to trial. Ultimately, the decision to go to trial will be yours. We will never tell you that you have to go to trial. We will tell you the pros and cons, as well as the risks and potential rewards of proceeding to trial. The ultimate decision as to whether or not you go to trial is yours and yours alone.

Q: Why Would My Case Go To Trial?

Your case would go trial because you choose to go to trial and the insurance company has not made an acceptable settlement offer. You will be given all of the necessary information to make this decision. Your attorney will be available to answer any questions you may have before you make the decision. It should be noted that your attorney may not take a case to trial or may advise against going to trial if it has been determined that it is not economically feasible to do so.

Q: Why Isn't The Insurance Company Simply Being Fair?

The insurance company is not in the business of insurance to be fair and pay claims. The more money the insurance company pays out, the less money the insurance company makes.

Q: If I Decide To Go To Trial, Do I Get To Sue The Insurance Carrier?

No. In most situations, you are prohibited by the laws of the State of Oklahoma from naming an insurance carrier as a party Defendant. You must sue the responsible party, not their insurance carrier. In fact, in Oklahoma you are prohibited from even mentioning insurance at trial. If you mention insurance at trial it is possible a judge will grant a mistrial and you could be responsible for the other side's attorney fees and costs. The Oklahoma legislature has said that whether or not a person carries insurance is not relevant to the facts of the underlined case. This hurts the Plaintiff in most situations. For example, the jury may feel sorry for the Defendant thinking the

Defendant has to pay out of their own pocket. In most circumstances, a Defendant will never have to pay anything. In fact, if a Plaintiff gets an excess verdict, over and above a Defendants insurance policy, it is likely that the Defendant's insurance carrier will pay the entire verdict even if the judgment is more than the policy limits of the Defendant.

Q: If We Go To Trial, Will The Jury Know That There Is Insurance To Pay The Verdict?

No. In Oklahoma, a jury is not permitted to hear whether or not the defendant has insurance. Business and insurance companies have done an excellent job of lobbying our legislature and getting judges to rule insurance is not relevant at trial. Hardly ever does a Defendant have to pay money out of their own pocket. However, the jury is not privy to this information. The jury for all we know believes that the Defendant has to pay this money out of his or her own pocket. That is not so. We would hardly ever consider taking a case to trial unless there was insurance. The reasons for that are because of the time, effort, and expense it takes to take a case to trial. We have to weigh whether or not there is a chance, or a likelihood, we will recover those costs, attorney fees, and expenses. If there is no insurance, it is more likely than not that all of the time and expense put into a case would never be recouped. Rarely would a Defendant have to pay anything out of his own pocket. In fact, if a Defendant ever has to pay something out of his own pocket, it is quite possible his may have a lawsuit against their own insurance carrier for what is called bad faith, for not settling the case within their policy limits.

Q: Will You Pursue A Case If There Is Not Any Insurance?

Probably not, but there have certainly been instances where we have taken a case when there is no insurance. It would depend on the case and the ability of the defendant to pay. Most people are judgment proof. What that means is if someone causes harm to you, and, if they do not have insurance, it is likely that you will never see a penny from them. Most assets that average individuals have are exempt by attachment from the judgment. What that means is if there is no insurance, it is likely we will not take your case. If a case goes to trial, it is more likely than not there is an insurance policy to pay for the damages the jury awards.

Q: What If My Health Insurance Carrier Has Paid My Medical Expenses? What Happens Then?

If you collect money from the Defendant, you will probably have to pay your health insurance carrier back.

Q: Who Hires The Lawyer That Represents The Defendant?

The Defendant's insurance carrier pays for the lawyer representing the Defendant. Sometimes the lawyer representing the Defendant is even an employee of the Defendant's insurance carrier. The jury will never know this information. The jury is likely to believe the Defendant is paying for that lawyer out of his own pocket. This is not so. In all reality, the Defendant is not charged anything for his defense.

Q: How Much Will It Cost To Take My Case To Trial?

Thousands and thousands of dollars. The type of case it is and the complexity of the case determines how much it will cost to take your case to trial. If your case is a simple rear end collision car wreck case, it is likely we will spend somewhere in the neighborhood of $10,000-$20,000 preparing your case for trial. If your case is a trucking wreck, product liability, medical malpractice, or complex case, it is likely we will spend an excess of $150,000-$200,000 preparing your case for trial.

Q: Who Is The Doctor The Defendant Uses At Trial?

More likely than not, it will be a doctor who has been hired by the insurance company or the defense attorney many times in the past. There are certain doctors that are hired to perform these functions. Most doctors will not do this type of work since they are usually busy helping patients and do not have the time. These defense doctors make a living by writing reports for the insurance company helping them attempt to reduce the amount of money the insurance company has to pay a Plaintiff. These doctors are biased and prejudiced, and will say whatever it takes in order to win a case. They are hired to render "opinions." Remember, a doctor can have an opinion that makes no sense at all. Even if he is wrong, it is just his opinion. They are professional testifiers and they can handle the courtroom. They have testified hundreds and thousands of times across the state of Oklahoma and they get paid to minimize the amount the insurance company has to pay a Plaintiff.

Q: What Is A Deposition?

A deposition is a statement given under oath, usually taken in a lawyer's office or a court reporting firm, before a court reporter. Witnesses called to testify in a deposition answer questions posed by the attorneys representing both parties in a case. The court reporter produces a written transcript of everything said at the deposition, and the witnesses read and sign the transcript swearing it to be an accurate statement of the evidence given under oath.

Q: What Should I Wear To Depositions, Court or Mediation?

People commonly ask me what they should wear during depositions, mediation or court proceedings, and I simply say wear what's comfortable. You want to look presentable and respectable, but you don't need to dress up as if you're going to a wedding or church. What I might recommend to one person would possibly make another person uncomfortable. I would suggest dressing as if you were going to a job interview. Some people wear jeans and a nice shirt and other wear a suit and tie. The main thing is we want you comfortable. Always know that people are watching and judging you, whether it be the mediator, opposing counsel, or jury. First impressions matter, so try to make a good one.

Q: What Is A Contingent Fee?

A fee is contingent when it is conditioned upon your attorney's successfully resolution of your case. It is often referred to as: "No fee unless you win." However, the client is generally responsible for the "out-of-pocket" costs of litigation (which most of the time will be waived if the case is lost). A Contingent Fee is paid as a percentage of your monetary recovery.

Q: Should I Provide A Statement To An Insurance Company Without A Lawyer Help?

No. The more significant your injuries, the more important it is to seek legal counsel before talking to an insurance company. The insurance company may try to diminish the significance of your injuries or talk you into taking a settlement below what you deserve. It would be detrimental to provide an incomplete statement early in the process until you and your attorney know the details and severity of your injuries. You should have your attorney present if you give a statement to an insurance adjuster or lawyer for the insurance company. This will ensure you are properly protected and there are no improper questions asked.

Q: What's The Difference Between An Injury Causing Accident And A Personal Injury Case?

The primary difference between accidents that cause injury and personal injury cases is that the latter is caused by negligence of another party. This can be a driver not paying attention, doctor's failure to properly diagnose a disease, a product manufacturer's forgetting to place a warning label on a product, a property owner's inadequacy to maintain safety standards, etc.

Q: Do I Have A Case If I Do Not Feel Hurt?

You may still have a case even if you do not feel hurt at the scene. The biological response to a traumatic situation like an accident sends a rush of adrenaline through the body, which can temporarily reduce sensations of pain. You may start feeling significant pain or developing other symptoms later. It is wise to consult a doctor even if you do not feel immediate, excruciating pain, since some of the most serious conditions emerge over time; sometimes, even days or weeks after an event.

Q: Are Auto Accidents The Only Type Of Personal Injury?

No. Auto accidents are the most common type of personal injury recognized by the general public. Along with auto accidents, personal injury law also includes home accidents, boat accidents, airplane crashes, dog bites, defective products, failure to provide adequate security, and malpractice, including the failure to diagnose, to name a few.

Q: What Should I Do If An Adjuster From The "At-Fault" Driver's Insurance Company Calls Me?

Do not speak with the adjuster. Refer the adjuster to your attorney. Also, do not speak with the attorney for the "at-fault" driver. These are highly trained individuals who are trying to speak with you to either beat your case or minimize what their employer has to pay you. They may even be recording you without your knowledge.

Q: How Long Will It Take To Settle My Claim?

There is no set answer. All cases are different. The more complex the case, the longer it takes to settle. If you have substantial injuries, the longer it will take. The more money there is at stake for the insurance company, the longer it will take. In most cases, the settlement process starts when your doctor releases you from treatment. Assuming your attorney has all of your accident-related records, your claim could be filed with the insurance company in five to ten business days. It may take the adjuster four to six weeks to evaluate your claim and make an initial offer. At this point, it's a matter of both sides negotiating a dollar amount that is reasonable for your case and acceptable to you. If you receive medical treatment for two to four months, it is possible your claim could be settled within six months. Most of the time, for a simple clear liability case, it will take between 6 to 12 months to settle your case. However, if the case is more complex, or if there are disputes as to liability or damages, it could take years to complete your case.

Q: What Are My Property Damage Rights In A Car Wreck?

The duty of the insurance company for the "at-fault" driver is to put you back in the place you were in immediately before the accident. You are entitled to have your car repaired to its pre-accident condition or receive its "fair market value" if your car is totaled. If your vehicle is totaled, the question then becomes what is the fair market value of the vehicle. The insurance companies spend a ton of money on computer programs designed to minimize what they have to pay. You may have to talk to a used car dealership to determine if their "fair market value" is really the fair market value. If your vehicle is not totaled (i.e. it's repairable), the insurance company must pay for the repairs.

Q: Is It Okay To Post Things About My Case On Social Media?

Do not post anything about your case on social media (Facebook, Twitter, Instagram, etc.). Many cases have been lost, or severely damaged, as a result of a client posting or saying something trying to be funny or simply not understanding how a defense attorney would twist their statements or intent. I advise all clients to be very careful with what they post and to enable their privacy settings. Before you post something ask yourself whether or not it would embarrass you if it were posted on the front page of the local paper. Another example of how this can hurt you is if you claim to be injured as a result of your claim and you post a picture of yourself doing a handstand, water skiing, running a marathon, etc. Photos like these will ultimately kill your case.

Q: Is There Ever A Guarantee I Will Win My Case?

There are never any guarantees you will win or lose your claim. We cannot and will not guarantee the result we achieve will be the result you may desire. There is no way to predict what a jury will do when it makes its decision. The laws concerning most cases are written in a manner where a jury can do whatever it believes is right. The question then becomes what will a jury think is right? No one can predict what a jury thinks is right. The only promises we can give you are that we will work hard for you, be honest with you, and properly prepare your case. To predict what a judge or jury may do with your case is virtually impossible.

RESULTS JOE CARSON HAS ACHIEVED FOR HIS CLIENTS

Name	Case Type	Case Information	Settlement Amount
Confidential	Insurance Class Action	It was alleged that the Insurance Company failed to pay benefits that were due under the insurance policies.	Settled for Approx. $12,000,000.00
Confidential	Environmental Class Action	It was alleged that Plaintiff's ground water was contaminated by Defendant's actions on nearby property.	Settled for Approx. $30,000,000.00
Confidential	Aviation	It was alleged that a private jet pilot failed to properly announce his approach at an uncontrolled airport. Because of the landscape and conditions of the airport, it was necessary to follow proper recommended approach procedures. A collision occurred at the intersection of two runways as Plaintiff attempted to takeoff. Plaintiff was killed.	Settled for Approx. $3,500,000.00
Confidential	Aviation	This case involved a helicopter crash where it was alleged that the pilot was acting in an unsafe manner and made certain mistakes that caused the helicopter to crash. Plaintiff sustained serious personal injuries.	Settled for Approx. $3,000,000.00
Vincent v. Consolidated Lumber Transport	Trucking	A semi-truck passing through Oklahoma failed to properly secure a load. As the driver was traveling down the highway, part of the load came off the trailer. Plaintiff struck the load and sustained a low back injury and underwent a one level fusion.	Jury returned a verdict of $1,147,932.00 for compensatory damages and $1,147,932.00 in punitive damages

Confidential	Trucking	A semi-truck failed to stop at a stop sign and struck the vehicle in which the client's husband was a passenger. He was killed on impact.	Settled for Approx. $9,500,000.00
Willis v. Sawatzky Construction	Trucking	Plaintiff was a truck driver that swerved to miss another truck that came into his lane. The plaintiff left the roadway and his tractor turned over. Plaintiff injured his shoulder in the wreck and had to have rotary cuff surgery as a result of the injury.	Jury returned a verdict of $1,506,000.00
Confidential	Auto Wreck	A van with six individuals from Guatemala and Mexico were traveling through Oklahoma on their way to work when a vehicle crossed the center line and struck them head-on killing 5 and injuring the other. Attorneys for Defendants alleged the Defendant had a heart attack and died before he crossed the center line and therefore there was no negligence.	Settled for a confidential amount, but the surviving spouses in Guatemala and Mexico should never have to work again.
Confidential	Trucking	A semi-truck driver was backing a flatbed trailer from a private drive early one morning when Plaintiff, traveling down the same road, struck the trailer in her lane of traffic at the speed limit. Plaintiff alleged the trailer was dirty and the side lights did not work. Plaintiff injured her neck and required a one level neck fusion.	Settled for Approx. $1,500,000.00
Confidential	Medical Malpractice	Plaintiff alleged that her doctor failed to diagnose	Settled for Approx. $750,000.00

		cervical cancer and failed to properly follow up resulting in her diagnosis of cervical cancer.	
Confidential	Medical Malpractice	Plaintiff presented to the ER three days in a row complaining of abdominal issues. On the first two visits, the plaintiff was misdiagnosed with gas and constipation. However, on the third visit, the ER finally admitted her and ran tests. It turned out that she had an infection that was killing her colon, and the plaintiff had to have her colon removed. Plaintiff alleged that had the ER properly diagnosed her on the first or second visit she would not have lost her colon.	Settled for Approx. $650,000.00
Confidential	Medical Malpractice	Plaintiff alleged that her doctor took the wrong approach when performing a thoracic back surgery. Due to the doctor's treatment, the spinal cord was stretched during the procedure which resulted in limited use of her lower extremities.	Settled for Approx. $750,000.00
Degiusti v. Valuck	Medical Malpractice	Plaintiff alleged that a doctor over prescribed opioid medications and failed to take a proper history and monitor labs. As a result, Plaintiff suffered kidney damage and will likely be required to have a kidney transplant or go on dialysis in the future. Plaintiff alleged that had the doctor paid attention to Plaintiff's preexisting health	$11,842,679.00 Compensatory Damages $12,000,000.00 Punitive Damages Total of $23,842,679.00

		conditions and properly monitored the treatment the injury would not have occurred. Additionally, Plaintiff alleged that the doctor was running a pill mill.	
Confidential	Medical Malpractice	Plaintiff presented to her family physician with stroke like symptoms, and the doctor examined and released her to go home. Approximately 1 hour later, she had a stroke which caused her to lose some function on her left side. Plaintiff alleged that she should have been given a clot buster drug when she first presented to her doctor.	Settled for Approx. $800,000.00
Confidential	Auto Wreck	Plaintiff was a passenger in a vehicle traveling below the speed limit on the highway when they were struck from behind and pushed off the road. The driver of plaintiff's vehicle died as a result of the injuries. Plaintiff sustained numerous broken bones and stayed in the hospital for approximately 3 days.	Settled for Approx. $1,750,000.00
Confidential	Product Liability	Plaintiff purchased a bench press style mechanical workout machine from a TV advertisement. As he was bench pressing, the bench collapsed causing the Plaintiff to sustain a neck injury which required a neck fusion. Plaintiff sued the manufacturer.	Settled for Approx. $750,000.00
Confidential	Product Liability	Plaintiff's father died because he was thrown from	Settled for Approx. $3,500,000.00

		the cab of his vehicle when he was struck by a semi-truck. The strike was a glancing blow that barely clipped his front bumper. Because of the impact, the cab separated and the seatbelt failed to properly secure the father in the cab. If he would have remained in the cab, it is alleged that he would not have been injured.	
Confidential	Product Liability	Decedent was a passenger in a UTV that went air born and rolled. It is alleged that the roll cage of the UTV was defective in that it did not properly protect the occupants of the UTV.	Settled for Approx. $1,000,000.00
Confidential	Oil Field Injury	Plaintiff was unloading pipe from a trailer when the pipe started to fall from the trailer and crushed him to death.	Settled for Approx. $3,500,000.00
Lounds v. Oklahoma VA	Nursing Home Negligence	Daughter alleged that when her father went to live in the nursing home that the staff failed to properly evaluate him, failed to properly monitor him, and failed to provide care. He lost a significant amount of weight over a short period of time and nothing was done by the staff of the nursing home. Shortly thereafter he died.	Verdict of $175,000.00 (maximum amount allowed by law since it was a governmental entity)

Index

A

Ability to Collect · 28
at-fault party · 49
automobile accident · 21
aviation · 73

B

borrow money · 70

C

comparative damages state · 34
Comparative negligence · 33
complex medical negligence · 73
contingency fee · 73
CT scan · 24

D

Damages · 28
Daubert challenges · 66
defense attorneys · 33
deposition · 96
discovery · 59

E

exaggerate · 68

I

Insurance companies · 50
interrogatories · 59
investigators · 77

L

lawsuit · 53
Liability · 27
lien · 37

limine · 66
Lyft · 42

M

mediation · 61
medical malpractice · 66
medical records · 75
MedPay · 42
mental anguish · 17
Modified Comparative Negligence · 34
MRI · 24

O

Oklahoma Highway Safety Office · 15

P

Personal injury law · 14
plaintiff · 64
preexisting medical condition · 30
pretrial motions · 65
product liability · 73
Punitive damages · 35

R

reconstructionists · 77

S

settlement · 69
social media · 102
statute of limitations · 25

T

third-party medical practitioner · 37
tortfeasor · 40
trial · 58

U

Uber · 42
uninsured motorist policy · 40

NOTES

Made in the USA
Monee, IL
05 November 2026

67387503R00069